Old LANARK

by

Rhona Wilson

Lanimer Day. 1913. Daffodils.

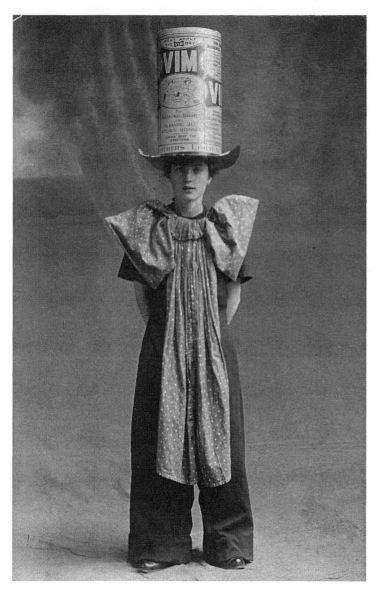

ACKNOWLEDGEMENTS

I'd like to thank the staff at Lanark Library who were extremely helpful throughout my research and also Betty and Fred Joynes. Thanks also to David Brown who checked my text.

FURTHER READING

Statistical Account of Scotland
New Statistical Account
Third Statistical Account
Anon, *Castlebank House*, series of notes at Lanark Library
Andrew Beveridge, *Clydesdale*, undated
John Butt et al, *Robert Owen of New Lanark*, 1971
Hugh Davidson, *Lanark Past and Present*, 1899
Hugh Davidson, *Lanark : A Series of Papers*, 1910
Ian Donnachie & George Hewitt, *Historic New Lanark*, 1993
Dorothy Haynes, *Lanark in Old Picture Postcards*, 1983
Dorothy Haynes, *Royal Burgh of Lanark Commemorative Brochure*, 1974
Patrick Mileham, *The Yeomanry Regiments*, 1994
A D Robertson, *Lanark and its Councils*, 1974
Keith Sanders & Douglas Hodgins, *British Railways Past and Present*, 1995
John Thomas, *A Regional History of the Railways*, 1984
St Mary's Church Souvenir Brochure, 1910

© Stenlake Publishing 1998
First published in the United Kingdom, 1998,
reprinted 2003, 2007, 2009, 2011
by Stenlake Publishing Limited
01290 551122
www.stenlake.co.uk

ISBN 9781840330199

All dressed up as a tin of scouring powder for Lanimer Day celebrations.

Introduction

Lanark was a place of political significance in the past, and not just to Scottish or English kings. It appears under the name of Colonia on a Roman map (Ptolemy's Map) dating from AD 120. In 978 Lanark proper received its first mention in historical records when Kenneth II used the town as a venue for an assembly or parliament. Other references to it are scattered across the centuries, many in connection with events or places which are claimed as part of Lanark's history but can no longer be proven as such. Castle Hill was supposedly the site of Lanark Castle in the past, but since no structural evidence remains, we must accept a thirteenth century treaty whereby a 'Castle of Lanark' was mortgaged to provide financial incentive for a political marriage, as proof of its existence. Similarly, William the Lion spoke about Lanark as his burgh, but since no charter exists from this time we must credit Alexander I with elevating Lanark to burgh status.

There was no doubt, however, as to when New Lanark made its mark on Scotland's industrial map. David Dale started building by the Clyde in 1785, put off neither by the wild state of the location, the fire that burned down his first mill or the difficulties in procuring employees for, what was initially, a highly unpopular way to earn a living. Just six years later there were almost 1,000 people working at his cotton mills, the figure soaring to over double that by the 1840s. The village quickly became a tourist attraction for Victorians interested firstly in the factory concept and then pleasantly scandalised by the socialist ideas of Robert Owen, Dale's son-in-law. Water power was the parish's principal asset, however, and Lanark was excluded from the burgeoning of heavy industry elsewhere in Lanarkshire by its lack of natural resources. The moor was searched fruitlessly for coal in the 1690s, 1750s and 1840s, and a small silver mine in Breadle proved unworkable.

Despite the arrival of Dale's mills, agriculture and weaving remained the staple occupations of the townspeople. New crops such as the potato and the turnip were introduced, although some complained that the former ruined their soil. Enclosure of fields by hedges was becoming more frequent by the 1790s and a few thirty-eight year leases (a working lifetime) were handed out to farmers in the 1770s to encourage them to improve their lands. The main problem was that the rapid growth of the mills meant that demand for produce outstripped supply, and goods had to be brought in at higher costs from neighbouring towns.

By contrast, the weavers' tale is more one of decline than prosperity. By the 1840s Lanark's 800 weavers were living in near destitution because of falling prices, 'hardly [able to] procure sufficient food', in the words of their minister. The town's last handloom weavers died in the twentieth century but the industry was finished long before then.

Overall, the twentieth century has been kind to Lanark. Its population never experienced the rapid growth of the steel towns, and never suffered the losses which accompanied the industry's subsequent collapse. Like those in Catrine, Dale's mills survived into their third century, ultimately under the management of the Gourock Ropeworks. The town became known for its textile factories, its cattle market and as a shopping centre for the surrounding district. These days it is benefiting from an influx of tourists, attracted by the restoration of the mills, a long term (and at some points seemingly hopeless) task, instigated several years after they were finally closed in 1968. The New Lanark Association now manages a lengthy waiting list for homes in the village, which had a total of just eighty inhabitants in the 1970s.

Perhaps the most significant proof of Lanark's survival as a community, however, is the continuing celebration of Lanimer Day. Since the First World War the old pillars of village life – the village band, gala days and the summer day trip – have slowly died out. For Lanark's centuries-old festival to survive and even expand (the day has become a week, the simple horse-drawn carts now replaced by fantastic creations aboard lorries) is truly surprising. Despite losing its council and provost as a result of regionalisation in the seventies, the town continues to show the sense of identity it did when Lanimer Day consisted of no more than following the town magistrates around as they checked the burgh's boundary stones. This ritual is still carried out today, encouraging in Lanarkians a strong sense of community, unusual in our time.

HIGH STREET LANARK

Originally more a district than a street, High Street was known as Hieton until the eighteenth century. In fact the only town names which have stayed the same over the years are those of Bloomgate, Broomgate, Castlegate and Wellgate. Ninety feet wide in some places, High Street had a clear stream, 'The Puddin' Burn', running down its centre until the town council decided to cover it and convert it into a sewer in the 1830s. Despite protests the council had its way and enclosed the Puddin', which still bubbles under High Street today. During the 1940s the street's broad expanse was divided down the middle with concrete blocks, referred to by the unimpressed as being like 'tombstones and sharks' teeth'. These days the look has been improved by the addition of trees and shrubs and High Street has developed into a very busy thoroughfare.

Lanark's original parish church was the twelfth century St Kentigern's chapel where William Wallace was married, a short distance south-east of town. St Nicholas' was built initially as a pendicle of it in the early 1770s, and was known as the 'in' church to St Kentigern's 'oot' (out of town) church. When the parent church fell into disrepair the congregation transferred to the town church. St Nicholas' steeple belongs to the council who built it to hold St Kentigern's old bell, which, if the inscription dated AD 1110 on its rim is anything to go by, is one of the oldest in Europe. The Jubilee Fountain at the cross stood in its original position (above) for only ten years before the council started to dither about where to keep it. Off it went to the horse market and then back to the High Street and once more to the horse market until the officials dismantled it altogether. More startling was the opinion expressed in the demolition-happy seventies that the church was 'in the way' of traffic and should be removed.

There is some dispute over the origins of Lanark's name, and no single derivation stands out as being distinctly linked to the town or its environs. A historian of the 1790s claimed that locals pronounced it Lanerick or Landerick (certainly one tradition that hasn't survived into the twentieth century) and that it was derived from the Gaelic *lan* meaning land, house or church and *dearc* meaning bilberry or blaeberry. 'Land of the bilberries' doesn't quite ring true, but we fare no better with the Latin *lana arca* put forward in the 1840s and meaning 'the wool chest'. My preferred choice would be either *lan aerig* meaning 'the bank of a river' or *lan arc*, the way the name was apparently spelled in old charters, meaning 'full ark' or 'granary'. Few historians question the naming of New Lanark but it seems strange that neither Dale nor Owen gave this built-from-scratch community its own village name.

Handing over Standard to new Lord Cornet Lanimer 1937.

This unusual view looks down Castlegate from the bottom of High Street on one of Lanark's many ceremonial occasions. There are conflicting stories about the origins of the stone dogs on top of one of the buildings in Castlegate. A sad tale of a cherished pet dog being run over and commemorated in stone was mentioned to me but I prefer the story relating to Vere House. Built in Castlegate in 1650, Vere House had a Miss Inglis in residence by the nineteenth century who nursed a particular hatred for a neighbour's dog. John Macdonald was in the process of building his house a little further down the street and Miss Inglis took such exception to his pet that it was put down. In revenge he had a statue of his dog made and positioned the snarling likeness on his roof so as to grimace directly into Miss Inglis's favourite window for sitting at.

There's no evidence that Lanark was ever surrounded by a wall, but it certainly had four town gates to guard against intruders. West Port was one of them and this part of town dates back to the thirteenth century, although the order from the town council stating that there should be four ports only dates from the 1680s. The other strongholds were at East Port, Wellgate and Castlegate, the gate at West Port stretching across the road at the opening of North Vennel and Friar's Lane. West Port gate was demolished in the 1770s as society became more civilised, its stones recycled in houses at Kingson's Knowe (no longer on the map). These days West Port is remembered in a street of the same name tacked on to the end of Bloomgate.

ORIGINAL ITALIAN ICE CREAM.

S. MINCHELLA

ITALIAN ICE CREAM SALOON

Pictures of the Minchella family at work and play around Lanark are fairly common. There was even a series of postcards of Maria Rosa Minchella printed when she became an exotic-looking Lanimer Queen in 1907. In this picture the family stands outside their cafe at No. 29 Wellgate in 1896, according to details written on the back of the photograph by Mrs Caroline Minchella. This information has been strongly disputed by some locals, however, who claim that it is actually a picture of the larger shop they moved to in Bannatyne Street. It's difficult to work out the truth of the matter since the Wellgate site has been demolished and replaced by modern flats built in 1994.

1820

The Minchella family again, this time by the old sawmills in Bannatyne Street and just about to set off for a picnic at Tinto Hill. Their Bannatyne Street Asiago Cafe was commissioned by Steven Minchella and opened around 1912. When this picture was taken Steven's son Angelo was apparently involved in the war in Italy as a dispatch rider. On his return, and after his father's death, he ran the family business together with his sister Caroline. Bannatyne Street (previously known as the Roddings) got its new name after some of its houses were built on land acquired from John Bannatyne of Castlebank House.

WELLGATE, LANARK

Wellgate, along with Cross Keys Close, apparently once contained some examples of Flemish architecture. The town was an established market for goods such as wool, hides and butter. Flemish mercantile colonies, protected by special laws, developed in the town, as well as elsewhere in Scotland. There is a tradition that Lanark was the first place in Scotland to partake of a cup of tea, courtesy of these old trade links. A Sir Andrew Kennedy is supposed to have passed on a gift of tea from the Dutch East India Company to friends in Lanark. If he did, he was no doubt cursed the length and breadth of the country since the beverage was considered an abomination when it first began to appear in the front rooms of the better off. Until the early eighteenth century ale and whisky were far more socially acceptable beverages, even at breakfast time, and there are various hilarious accounts of people taking vows of abstinence against the milder drink in case it weakened their constitution.

11

Wellgate-Head looks much the same today, with the Gusset House still intact. This postcard was sent by a collector, apparently with an ulterior motive. 'Dear Marion,' the back reads, 'Got your letter all right. Glad to hear from you again. We've been staying at Lanark for a week. Go home tomorrow. Will write after we get home. Send a card soon – I'm as daft for them as ever.' In the past, holidays for working families were confined mostly to day trips. If they did have time to go away they would visit a relative, often in the country, and Lanark, still pretty today, seems a sensible choice of location. This was more likely a matter of chance than design, however, since people went happily 'on holiday' to all manner of Scottish towns. Bellshill, Wishaw and Shotts were just a few of the industrial beauty spots used as holiday locales and considered as popular as the Costa del Sol by visitors glad of the chance to get out of the polluted cities.

BANNATYNE STREET, LANARK

D 2040

Lanark's Co-op, established by a group of weavers in 1862, has been replaced by an Oxfam charity shop since this picture was taken. Co-ops began to spring up after the Napoleonic Wars when the weaving industry went into recession. The post-strike rate of 6d a web was considered too low to earn a living from, but by the late 1830s weavers in Lanark were lucky to get 1½d for some pieces. With an average wage of just six shillings a week (not counting deductions of a shilling or two for hire of the loom and so on) it was possible to survive only if you kept to a strict budget and had several family members attending the loom. The few who managed to earn more did so at the expense of their health, which was quickly ruined by sitting at the loom for some sixteen hours a day.

STATION SQUARE, LANARK

St Leonard's Street, home to Station Square, was named after the ancient St Leonard's Hospital, which once stood at the top of the street. Robert III granted Sir John Dalzell the rights to the revenue from the hospital and its lands in the early 1390s on condition that he and his heirs provided a mass for his children once every seven years in perpetuity. The hospital's ruins survived until the 1790s, although all traces of them are now gone. St Leonard's Church, left, was erected in 1842, although Mr Stark (its minister) and his supporters walked out during the Disruption the following year. Although he had seceded from the Church of Scotland the minister still wanted to use its church and took part in an unsuccessful lawsuit to try and secure this right. By the late 1960s St Leonard's dwindling congregation had agreed to merge with the parish church which took on the name of St Nicholas, leaving the Station Square building empty. St Leonard's was demolished in the mid-seventies and replaced by modern buildings.

St Leonard's Church, Lanark

Brown's Series.

In 1855 the privately owned Lanark Railway constructed a line from Cleghorn, on the main line north of Carstairs, to Lanark, making it possible to run services to Glasgow and Edinburgh. The line was acquired by the Caledonian Railway in 1860, and was doubled in length to reach Douglas a few years later. The early 1870s saw it open for goods traffic at Muirkirk where the Caledonian line linked up to the Glasgow and South Western Railway line from Auchinleck. This began carrying passengers the following year. A trade dispute in Muirkirk caused a fall in numbers in the early twenties which led to its eventual closure. Today all that's left is the line from Lanark Junction to Lanark Station.

During Lanimer Day (now Lanimer Week, held in early June) Lanark's streets are transformed by bunting, floats, processions and ceremonies. The celebrations have been held since the twelfth century, the pre-Reformation festival thought to be linked to the ancient Corpus Christi Festival. In the beginning Lanimer Day was simply the day designated by the town magistrates for their annual check of the town boundary stones. They set off at 5 a.m. and the townspeople began to join them, despite the unholy hour, until the inspection became a full-blown procession. In the 1840s the ancient custom was threatened when participants stripped bark from trees along the route to wave in the air. In later years saplings were pulled up, and this led to a dispute with the owner of the Jerviswood Estate, who complained about the damage done to his woodlands.

The crowning of Maria Rosa Minchella, Lanimer Queen 1907. Due to disputes with the Jerviswood Estate, the boundary stones were inspected by Lanark town magistrates alone from 1848 to 1850, although the townspeople were allowed to join in once again at a later date. During the nineteenth century the ritual took on new significance, particularly for Lanark's male population. Men and boys were encouraged to celebrate their first Lanimer inspection by being dunked in the water at the Lockhart Bridge boundary stone. Later, coins were thrown in shallow water to provide some fun for those children who were taking part.

America's Prohibition years were obviously an influence on the creators of this float; nowadays, the extended opening hours of Lanark's pubs act as a liquid incentive for some outsiders to attend the Lanimer celebrations. As lifestyles changed the early hour of the Lanimer inspection became inconvenient and the boundary stone walk was moved to an evening slot. It's not clear how the formal procession first began but the first Lanimer Queen was crowned in 1893 in a ceremony near the Co-op. This important aspect of the day later moved to the cross as attendance grew.

MORRIS DANCERS 1921.

Children line up ready to march in the procession, which begins in St Leonard's Street. One dubious story about why the children first donned costumes goes along the lines that in 1890 local drapers had too many aprons so gave them to all the school children . . . and the rest is history. The writer of the Third Statistical Account tells us that in the 1950s several of the old boundary stones still existed and were faithfully visited by the town council and attendants each year. The procession through the town was by then the pride and joy of the local schools. Floats, which 'in artistic beauty often surpass the much vaunted carnival processions of the French and Italian Rivieras' were designed by teachers and made by their pupils.

CAITHNESS ROW
NEW LANARK

When David Dale, a Glasgow linen merchant and banker, first feued the site of New Lanark village in 1784 it was described as a 'mere morais' with nothing going for it apart from the water power of the nearby Clyde. Luckily, that was all that was needed. Dale started building the first of four mills the following year and by the early 1790s was employing well over 1,000 people, many of them Highlanders. These were recruited from the emigrant ship *The Fortune*, which Dale intercepted when it stopped at Greenock due to bad weather. Getting any workers at all was difficult in the early days because mills had a reputation akin to that of workhouses. Their ideal employee was a widow with several quick and nimble children, and there were over thirty fitting such a description in the village in the 1790s. Larger-framed and less docile male workers were less of a necessity especially when inventions such as New Lanark's patent jennies did away with the need for their strength. Caithness Row, above, was one of the first tenement blocks to be built for the workers.

New Lanark passed to Robert Owen, Dale's son-in-law, in 1800. This was the start of an interesting phase, and the number of curious people signing the visitors' book soared as Owen made his socialist ideals and plans for running the mills plain. Another of his communal living projects in Bellshill was known as Babylon by outraged locals. Owen considered the mills, as he found them, to be badly run (Dale had only been loosely involved in their day-to-day management) with unwisely chosen employees; 'immoral' was just one of his criticisms in view of the fact that over 10% of births in the village were illegitimate. His first step was to increase the working hours, which was just about as popular as his drive to improve sanitation, consisting of compulsory house inspections by a team referred to scornfully as the Bug Hunters by local women. He was generous enough to continue to pay his workers in 1806 when an American export embargo stopped production, and his plan to build a school was welcomed by the workforce if not by his partners, who decided it was reason enough to dissolve the partnership.

Owen's ideas – that a happy workforce would be more productive and result in higher profits – were strangely threatening to the Victorian age. The village store, above, was one means of improving his workforce's standard of living and provided good quality goods at reasonable prices, but public attention seemed to focus more on Owen's personal morality such as the fact that he didn't believe in God. Perhaps the real fear was that such anti-establishment views could spread. One minister labelled Owen's seemingly ridiculous view that people could be 'good' and without 'impure thoughts' as a fantasy. By the mid-1820s a disillusioned Owen had left the mills enthused by a new project in Harmony, USA.

ROBERT OWEN'S LABOUR CHEQUE.

New Lanark wages cheque. In 1903 the Gourock Ropeworks bought the mills to produce netting yarns for weaving at Greenock. The new owners were popular employers according to a 1950s historian – there were no strikes because of the good relationship they had with their employees and villagers enjoyed the benefits of free electricity and no rates. Despite this, the mills and village were falling into disrepair by the 1960s. Certainly, about 75% of the village was neither employed by the Gourock Ropeworks nor related to those who were. The company offered the site to the council for £250 in 1962 but it refused the offer on account of the massive restoration costs. It was left to the New Lanark Association to begin the modernisation programme later taken up by a working party organised through the Scottish Civic Trust. Today the site has been turned into an impressive living monument, its museums tempered by the fun Annie McLeod Experience which involves a guided tour courtesy of a hologram ghost.

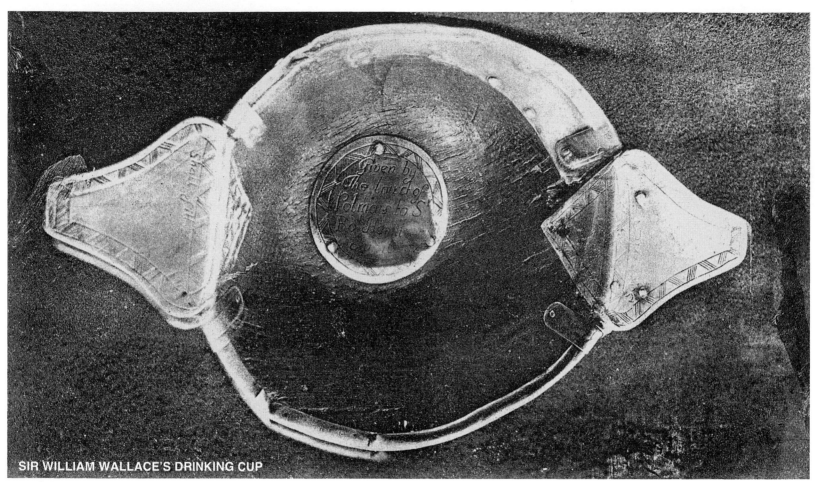

SIR WILLIAM WALLACE'S DRINKING CUP

Lanark has a long-standing connection with William Wallace, some of the references plausible, much of the detail dubious. Wallace married Marion Braidfute at Kentigern Chapel in 1296 and is said to have lived with her afterwards in a house in Castlegate. One day he got involved in a scuffle with Lanark's Sheriff, William Hesilrig, and ran to his home first before fleeing to the Cartland Crags. Depending on whom you read, Wallace may have had to contend with the sheriff's son as a rival for Marion's hand. Hesilrig put Marion to death as revenge and got himself and 200 (some say 40) English soldiers killed in turn by Wallace. Wallace's 'Drinking Cup' has a poem in reference to the hero engraved around the silver rim but it is unlikely that it carried water to his lips. The cup was owned by Lanark's Ross family, along with other artefacts including Wallace's chair, only parts of which dated back to the fourteenth century.

Before the advent of the mills, tourism in Lanark centred around the spectacular Falls of Clyde. Some of the estate owners positively encouraged this, the Ross family for one allowing access to the Bonnington Estate and erecting a bridge for the purpose of viewing. Steps were cut into the rock to form a descent at Corra Linn although they were probably somewhat dangerous when this picture was taken during the big freeze of 1895. Another fall, Stonebyres Linn, was mentioned by one writer in the 1790s as providing a lot of amusement on account of the salmon trying to scale its eighty foot height. These days Corra Linn has been taken into service by what was initially the Bonnington Power Station, opened in 1928. Their main flow is channelled off to provide hydro-electric power leaving the falls a trickle of their former selves. The only way to see them as they were is to scan the local papers for announcements of station maintenance work during which they are allowed to flow freely.

Originally a swamp, Lanark Loch was created as a reservoir in the 1850s with the aim of relieving the town's chronic water problem. Water for domestic use was obtained from the town's wells until as late as 1870, giving rise to names such as Wellhead and Wellgate. In the late nineteenth century some of these were discovered to be contaminated and were closed, at which point the town attempted to move to the reservoir system. By the 1950s the new supplies from the Tinto Hills were inadequate once more because of the growing population, and the success of the thirsty tomato industry. At this time Lanark had to buy up to 200,000 gallons of water a day from the county supply whose pipes ran through town.

Lanark's water supply wasn't the only thing that needed improving. One writer stated that the town itself only developed a decent appearance around the 1780s with the introduction of a few slate roofs. Even by the 1840s the town jail was in such a state that it housed only prisoners 'de bonne volante' (of good character) who presumably could be trusted as too polite to escape. Oil lighting was introduced in the early 1770s but the gas system destined to replace it wasn't effective until the 1830s. The Gas Consumer Council eventually took over the gas works in 1871 and by the 1950s the Clyde Valley Electrical Power Company was claiming that it lit most of Lanark's homes. Dry closets disappeared at around the same time, with the development of a new sewage system.

Lake Pavilion, Lanark

By 1855 boating was allowed on Lanark Loch, and a pair of swans appeared later, donated by the Earl of Home. The pavilion and the small sweetie kiosk were built as the loch became more popular, but there were still complaints from visitors that there was nothing much to do once you arrived, let alone seats or proper paths to walk along. The loch's steam launch (illustrated on the previous two pages), looking much like a converted rowing boat, arrived in 1905 and there was talk of restoring the entire site in the twenties. It wasn't until the 1970s that big changes were made with the advent of the restaurant, pitch and putt, picnic site, paddle boat area and sailing club.

Lanark Curling Club has been in existence since the 1840s although it is a relative newcomer compared to the bowling green at Castlehill which was established c.1758. The former club seems to have been fairly active in the 1860s, getting planning permission to build a shelter for their stones and badgering the council about the state of the weeds at Lanark Loch.

The club house and first tee, Lanark Golf Course. The course was built on Lanark Moor, once a communal resource belonging to the Burghers of Lanark. In the 1740s the town magistrates tried to develop it by letting out small plots at its edge on fifty-seven year leases in the hope that the lands would be enclosed and improved. Unfortunately the scheme fell through because the plots were too far away from town and this part of the moor remained wild despite the incentives. The writer of the First Statistical Account discussed William Honeyman's feu of several hundred acres of the moor. There was obviously a local dispute going on with the deal opposed by 'a few burgesses' who thought that the moor couldn't be feued or sold without reference to their ancient pasture and fuel rights. Their historian didn't agree with them, stating that it was far more important that the moor was improved and citing Honeyman's considerable financial investment.

Lanark Golf Club was established on the moor in the early 1850s and had a mere six holes at first. Its development was slow but steady, with a club house built in the 1880s and the course extended to eighteen holes by 1896. The other prestigious sport in the area was horse racing, supposedly introduced by King William the Lion who set up an annual race. Legend has it that he also presented the Silver Bell prize competed for each autumn, although traces of a hallmark on the bell suggest it was made some time after 1485 when such marks were first introduced. Racing at Lanark stopped during Cromwell's puritanical crusade, and some believe the original bell was lost then and replaced when the sport recommenced in the early 1660s.

Scotland's first International Aviation Meeting was held at Lanark Racecourse in 1910, drawing crowds of more than 100,000 over the course of a week. At the time, flying was in its infancy and the meeting was a huge PR exercise aimed at convincing the public it was a viable means of transport. An aeroplane was a truly startling sight for most people, so facilities were organised on a large scale for the expected crowds and included a purpose-built rail station on the Racecourse. A special Aerodrome Post Office processed thousands of postcards, such as this one, from people who wanted to prove they'd been there. Twenty-three pilots competed in competitions for the highest altitude and the longest distance flown each day, with world records falling by the wayside. Captain Drexel charted a record altitude of 6,000 feet in his biplane one day although he managed to mistake Cobbinshaw Loch for Lanark Loch during the same flight. Drexel had to rely on more primitive means of transport to get himself out of his predicament, cycling to Cobbinshaw Station to wire for a lift.

Scottish International Aviation Meeting, Lanark.

The Lanark press went totally overboard on coverage, overjoyed by the prospect of an international event on its doorstep. Sometimes there was no news, but the column inches appeared anyway, one edition informing readers pointlessly that a seagull got a round of applause during a fallow period in the skies. Another expressed its satisfaction that 'all peepholes at the grounds have now been completely hidden' despite the fact that what was happening off the ground was much more interesting and visible for miles. Non-event headlines were rife. 'Aviator Unhurt' and 'Aviator Uninjured' seemed to echo the universal amazement that anyone could go up in these flimsy looking biplanes and make it down again. A Professor Biles of Glasgow, however, got a little more than he bargained for when he went up for a pleasure flight. Fifteen feet from the ground the wooden propeller broke and the plane crashed. A stiff upper lip was much in evidence in Biles' response to reporters' enquires about his flight: 'but for its awkward termination I have had a pleasant experience'.

AYRSHIRE YOEMANRY CAMP   LANARK 1909   (BROWN)

During the French Revolution, when a French invasion of Britain seemed a real possibility, voluntary yeomanry regiments were organised. The existing forces were small and inadequate and there were fears that some of the poorer sections of society might welcome the French because of poverty and unemployment. The militia, a conscripted force, was extremely unpopular so it was decided to assemble a prestigious volunteer force eventually known as the 'Gentlemen and Yeomanry Cavalry'. Gentlemen usually became officers whereas the rank and file was made up of tenant farmers and landowners. Each supplied his own horse and paid for his uniform and tack. In 1804 a 3,000-strong yeomanry force gathered near the Scottish border in an incident which became known as the 'False Alarm', showing the military's nerves. The troops were also used for other tasks such as suppressing riots, their aims being to preserve private property, the monarchy and, ultimately, the *status quo*.

Six troops of yeomanry had been raised in Lanarkshire by the mid-1860s. After the Boer War the government reorganised their defence strategy, forming the Territorial Force which took over many yeomanry regiments in 1908. The TF later became the Territorial Army, its members involved in many major wars. Volunteer regiments went abroad from 1914 because of manpower shortages and in early 1939 fears of a second world war brought about an announcement that the field force was to be doubled. In 1917 the Ayrshire and Lanarkshire Yeomanry amalgamated to form the Royal Scottish Fusiliers, serving in Palestine and France during World War I. Many of its members were lost in the Japanese invasion of Malaya in 1941. The Fusiliers went through various reformations until they went full circle, becoming the Lanarkshire and Glasgow Yeomanry Squadron of the Scottish Yeomanry in 1992.

A trooper posing outside the refreshment room at Lanark Market. In late eighteenth century Britain's relations with France were dire, and writers and historians could barely bring themselves to even call the country by her name. Instead, Lanark's First Statistical Account warned vaguely that, '*Anarchy* sits triumphant upon the *guillotine*, with *Murder* at her back and treading the rights of mankind under her feet'. Dickens used similar euphemisms in the opening pages of *A Tale of Two Cities*. Lanark residents had to face up to reality, however, in the 1811 to 1814 period when French POWs were stationed in the town. During the war the French sailed around Britain's coast harassing trade ships and, if captured in Scottish waters, they were taken to the dungeons at Edinburgh Castle. With over 1,000 ensconced there by the turn of the century it was decided to farm the prisoners out to be made use of in Scotland's small towns.

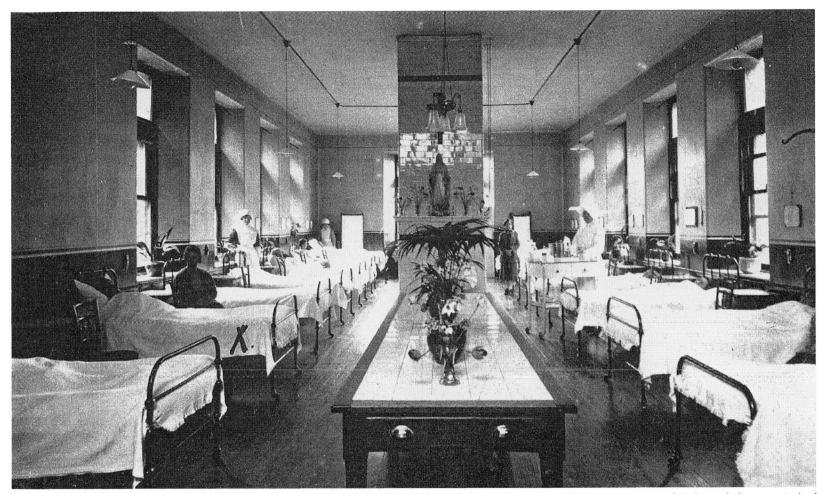

St John's Ward, St Mary's Hospital. At the beginning of the nineteenth century some thirty French soldiers were quartered in Lanark for a period of about two years. Some took up employment as teachers, which is how Robert Owen's sons learned French. The conditions of their internment seem to have been pretty lax since they had the run of the town and could travel within a five mile radius of it. Apparently the French prisoners were popular with Lanark's women who 'in some instances [lost] their virtue', something that was considered to have been a particular problem at New Lanark. A few, such as Captain Augustus Francis Brard, (who died in the early 1870s) married locally and settled in the town. These days Lanark has a far more positive connection with France in the light of its twinning with Yvetot in 1975.

Watering the horses. Of Lanark's three Statistical Accounts, the first one is perhaps the most interesting. 'Improve' seemed to be the Rev Wm Lockhart's favourite word, his preposterous enthusiasm for the new ideas of Scotland's improvers permeating every page. He uses the document as a platform for his plans for the parish's future: its land must be bettered, at any cost to old traditions, as must be the roads. The corn mill on the Mouse should be converted for flour production and the common moor must be tamed and taken advantage of. Despite this strident moralising, he couldn't resist flattering some heritors, and tells us that when the Lord Justice Clerk feued out the site of the mills he was 'influenced alone by the good of his country' – as opposed to the revenue.

The white lapels on these men's uniforms reveal that they are convalescing during the First World War. St Mary's Church prospered during the late nineteenth century amassing a congregation of over 1,000 attended by eleven priests. Built nearby in 1874, St Mary's Hospital was managed by the Sisters of Charity of St Vincent de Paul and was Lanark's first modern hospital. In later years the same order was involved in a boarding school for girls and the Smyllum Orphanage. The hospital was extended twice in the early twentieth century to provide beds for 100 patients.

This postcard, presumably of a young patient, is captioned 'St Mary's, Lanark'. The Third Statistical Account of the 1950s stated that despite the advent of the NHS, St Mary's was still a church concern run by the Sisters and financed by donations. A new hospital (of the same name) was built off Carstairs Road in the early 1970s whereby Lanark Town Council acquired the old one in the town centre, converting it into its District Council Office.

Lanark's mill was to the left of this pretty bridge which spans the River Mouse. Millers were generally rich but unpopular in the past because of their ancient right to a monopoly; burghers were obliged to get their corn ground at the town mill, regardless of whether they were happy with its service or not. During the nineteenth century the bridge was blithely described as 'Roman' (as were many other similarly designed bridges such as that in Strathclyde Park) although it is definitely not that old. Some historians believe that it was originally a wooden bridge with stone supports before being rebuilt in stone in the mid-seventeenth century. The New Statistical Account of the 1840s stated that when the new bridge (seen in the background) was built the old one was condemned. Michael Linning who lived nearby bought it to preserve it, however, although it was described as out of use and dangerous in the 1950s.

The remains of two Roman camps have been discovered in the Lanark area, the biggest close to Cleghorn House (above) and thought by General Roy to be the work of Agricola. The other camp was on the Lanark Moor on the opposite side of the river near to Carstairs. It was built at a later period and although it was smaller its remains are more distinct. Watling Street, the great Roman road which begins near Fleet Street, passes by the Mouse to the east of Cleghorn Bridge. A crannog (or lake dwelling) was also discovered on the Hyndford Estate in the late 1890s and examples of burial urns and Roman coins have turned up in various sites. Andrew Beveridge's poem Clydesdale (undated) states that its owner at that time was Captain Elliot Lockhart of Borthwickbrae in Selkirkshire. Its amenity had apparently just been injured by the building of the main line of the Caledonian Railway which passed by the front of the house.

Girls' Dining Hall, Smyllum Orphanage, Lanark.

Smyllum Park estate takes its name from Dr William Smellie, a famous obstetrician and its original owner, who built the mansion house and lived there until his death in the 1760s. The lands remained in his family for thirty years until they were sold to Sir William Honeyman (the unpopular improver of the moors) who extended the house considerably. Next came the Carmichael sisters who sold the estate to the Roman Catholic Church in the mid-1860s. The church founded an orphanage run by the Sisters of Charity from St Mary's, opening with a mere handful of children and an arduous task ahead. Umbrellas were needed over the beds when it rained at first because the house was in such a bad state of repair, and the estate lands had to be cultivated by the nuns to make the orphanage self-sufficient. Smyllum began to take in deaf and blind children (who were housed in separate buildings) in the 1880s and by the turn of the century had around 700 charges.

Boys' School, Smyllum Orphanage, Lanark.

In the twentieth century standards changed and a 1948 Social Services report found Smyllum House wanting. It was too big and had too many children, pictures like this one showing how they were really packed in. Many children were allocated to foster parents and by the enlightened mid-sixties dormitory style accommodation had vanished, the building instead divided into 'houses' of about twenty children with a sister in charge of each. Plans for closure announced in 1975 were finally realised in the early eighties and thereafter a succession of projects were discussed. In 1982 it was seen as a perfect home for the extended families of Vietnamese boat people, but the most serious bid was made by the Clyde Valley Christian Society. The society apparently bought Smyllum in the late eighties with a view to converting it into sheltered housing which caused a furore in the local press over the large grants the council offered. Today, however, the listed building stands in ruins and the orphanage itself has recently been the subject of an expose by the *News of the World* regarding the nuns' treatment of children in the past.

The origins of Lockhart Hospital's name lie in the ancient history of the family that built it. King Robert Bruce ordered that after he died his heart was to be taken to the Holy Land and Sir Simon Lockard was one of its protectors when the time came, changing the family name later to commemorate the occasion. During the journey he took prisoner a Saracen chief and managed to obtain his magic talisman (a triangular stone inset with a silver coin) as a ransom. Known as the Lee Penny after the family estates, legend tells us that it became famous for its medicinal properties – water which it had been dipped in could apparently cure ill cattle. This was taken so seriously at the time that a complaint against its superstitious use was heard by the Church Synod and Assembly. Lockhart Hospital -still standing today – was built by the Sir Simon Lockhart of the 1870s to fulfil his late brother's dream of a hospital in Lanark. It opened with just eighteen beds, and an annexe was later built to accommodate people injured in World War II's bombing raids, although it wasn't used much at the time.

Information relating to the history of Stanmore House is sparse and somewhat vague. A nineteenth century historian tells us that there was no sign of it on a map of 1815, adding that its later owner was 'his own ancestor and earned his position right worthily,' which presumably means he made his wealth as opposed to inheriting it. Robertson's account of the 1970s states that Robert and William Lithgow built the house as a boarding school for boys (Stanmore Academy) which survived for about thirty years. The Lithgows are also mentioned as being amongst the first members of the golf course which dates this information to the early 1850s. A century later Stanmore House had been converted into a residential school for handicapped children. Today the school helps children learn how to walk and talk using the 'conductive' techniques first developed at Hungary's famous Peto Institute.

Castlebank estate, known as Ninian's Bank in the fourteenth century, was bought by John Bannatyne in the eighteenth century. What happened in between is unclear and even the details of Bannatyne's purchase are dubious; it is not known whether the house existed when he bought the estate, although he is thought to have been in residence by the 1760s. The Bannatyne family went on to become very important in Lanark's political life, John senior being elected Provost in the late 1770s, a post he held for twenty years. After the Bannatynes left, records again become unclear. The next documented owner was Neil Dyce, Lanark's Sheriff Substitute, whose details appear on a valuation roll of the late 1850s. Castlebank remained in his family until the early 1880s when James Houldsworth, of the Coltness Iron Works in Wishaw, purchased the estate. He died in 1897 after which there are conflicting accounts about when his son took up residence; some say the 1890s, others 1904.

Employees at Castlebank House. It's not known when Castlebank's terraced gardens, one of the estate's main features, were first developed. An Ordnance Survey map of the mid-nineteenth century shows them clearly for the first time although there is an outline on Forrest's Map of 1813 which may show the gardens at an earlier stage. Whatever the case, the Houldsworths took great pride in Castlebank's grounds, improving then over the years by adding ornamental features such as the ponds, later filled in. In 1939 the estate was still private but opened to the general public (for a fee) under the Scottish Gardens Scheme. Just over twenty years later a notice of sale was published, with the schedule boasting twenty-six bedrooms and six bathrooms and inviting interested parties to attend the auction at the Clydesdale Hotel in August 1951. Lanark Town Council bought Castlebank House and lands, converting the former into flats and the latter into a free park for the townspeople.